KU-753-566

MAPPING

TOWNS & CITIES

BY
HOLLY DUHIG & MADELINE TYLER

BookLife
PUBLISHING

©2018
BookLife Publishing
King's Lynn
Norfolk PE30 4LS

All rights reserved.
Printed in Malaysia.

A catalogue record for this book is available from the British Library.

ISBN: 978-1-78637-323-6

Written by:
Holly Duhig & Madeline Tyler

Edited by:
Kirsty Holmes

Designed by:
Drue Rintoul

All facts, statistics, web addresses and URLs in this book were verified as valid and accurate at time of writing. No responsibility for any changes to external websites or references can be accepted by either the author or publisher.

Image Credits
All images are courtesy of Shutterstock.com, unless otherwise specified. With thanks to Getty Images, Thinkstock Photo and iStockphoto.
Front Cover – Dmitry Polonskiy, Rusla Ruseyn. 2 – oblong1. 4&5 – Artisticco, Alexander Lukatskiy, Anna Violet. 6&7 – Rainer Lesniewski, recreation of map originally from medium.com via briskat. 8&9 – george studio, Daniel Chetroni, Jaroslaw Kilian. 10&11 – Dmitry Kalinovsky, By Rama (Own work) [CeCILL (http://www.cecill.info/licences/Licence_CeCILL_V2-en.html) or CC BY-SA 2.0 fr (https://creativecommons.org/licenses/by-sa/2.0/fr/deed.en)], via Wikimedia Commons, Steven Bostock, Patryk Kosmider, Andrey Armyagov. Christian Wittmann. 12&13 – Peter Hermes Furian, Zivica Kerkez, Tomislav Pinter. 14&15 – Zoltan Major. 16&17 – Tish11, TierneyMJ, Fourleaflover. 18&19 – Art Berry, MarinaDa, By Alargule (Own work) [CC BY-SA 4.0 (https://creativecommons.org/licenses/by-sa/4.0), via Wikimedia Commons, Andrew Balcombe. 20&21 – rzoze19, By Sameboat (Own work) [CC BY-SA 4.0 (https://creativecommons.org/licenses/by-sa/4.0)], via Wikimedia Commons, Claudio Divizia, by ed g2s and James D. Forrester vis Wikimedia Commons. 22&23 – Neil Mitchell, By Ben Tesch [CC BY 2.0 (http://creativecommons.org/licenses/by/2.0), via Wikimedia Commons. 24&25 – Maxx-Studio, Maxger, Mio Buono, sevenMaps7, doyata, Makkuro GL. 26&27 – Thinglass, Michaelpuche, Lorelyn Medina, Engel Ching. 28&29 – chrisdorney, Pe3k, Tish1, By HistoryLV (Own work) [CC BY-SA 4.0 (https://creativecommons.org/licenses/by-sa/4.0)], via Wikimedia Commons. 30 – Kostenyukova Nataliya.

All facts, statistics, web addresses and URLs in this book were verified as valid and accurate at time of writing. No responsibility for any changes to external websites or references can be accepted by either the author or publisher.

CONTENTS

Words that look like **this** are explained in the glossary on page 31.

What Is a Map?

Maps are **diagrams** that show parts of the world and how they are connected. Maps can show a big area, like the entire world, or a small area, like a town or village. Some maps only show natural **features** of the landscape like mountains and rivers. Other maps show where buildings and roads are. Some maps only show specific areas. For example, amusement park maps help visitors find their way around the park and plan their day.

With this map a visitor can see where all the rides and rollercoasters are and how to get to each one.

CHOOSING WHAT TO MAP

Maps are a way of displaying information. Some maps, such as road maps, display information that helps people find their way from one place to another, but not all maps are made for travelling. Maps are also used to show information about **landmarks**, natural features, animals or people. A person who makes maps, called a cartographer, decides what to put on a map depending on the information the map is trying to show.

This map of Africa shows some natural features, such as vegetation, but not towns or cities.

BY NOT INCLUDING OTHER INFORMATION, THE MAP OF AFRICA IS EASIER TO READ.

GEOGRAPHIC MAPS

Different maps are used for different reasons. Maps of the climate show what sort of weather is expected for a certain time of year, whereas weather maps predict the weather for today or tomorrow. Road maps show drivers where to go, whilst a terrain map traces the rises and falls of the land. A political map shows the size of different countries and where the borders between them are. These types of maps are all geographic, which means they map the Earth and its features.

This is a map of the main roads between cities in the United States. Drivers can then use this map to plan the roads they'll need to travel from one city to another.

Non-Geographic Maps

There are even maps of objects and other things that aren't on the surface of the Earth. There are maps of space, such as solar system maps. There are tree-maps that show the order that things happened and how they are linked. For example, a family tree is an easy way to see how everyone in a family is related. Mind maps are ways to map ideas that are linked to one main topic.

Family tree

A family tree can map all the branches of a family.

MAPPING
LOCAL AREAS

Towns and cities are places where many people live together in a community. All these people need somewhere to live and somewhere to go to work or school, so towns and cities tend to be very big and have lots of buildings. As well as this, people need places to go and have fun such as cinemas, restaurants, theatres and shops; and places that keep them safe like police stations, fire stations and hospitals. The more people that live and work in an area, the more of these things will be needed. This is why some towns and cities can grow to be very large. New York is one of the largest cities in the world at over 780 kilometres (km) **squared**. Because it is so big, it is split into smaller areas called boroughs. These are: Manhattan, Brooklyn, Queens, Staten Island and The Bronx.

BRONX

NEW YOR

MANHATTAN

Hudson River

East River

Nass

La Guardia Airport

Hudson

ERSEY

QUEENS

Upper Bay

John F. Kennedy International Airport

BROOKLYN

Jamaica Bay

STATEN ISLAND

Lower Bay

NEW YORK IS SO BIG THAT THE NEW YORK POLICE DEPARTMENT HAVE OVER 70 POLICE PRECINCTS.

It is important to map towns and cities so that the people who live there, or tourists that have come to visit, know how to get around. Maps are great for giving directions, and they are useful for all sorts of other things too.

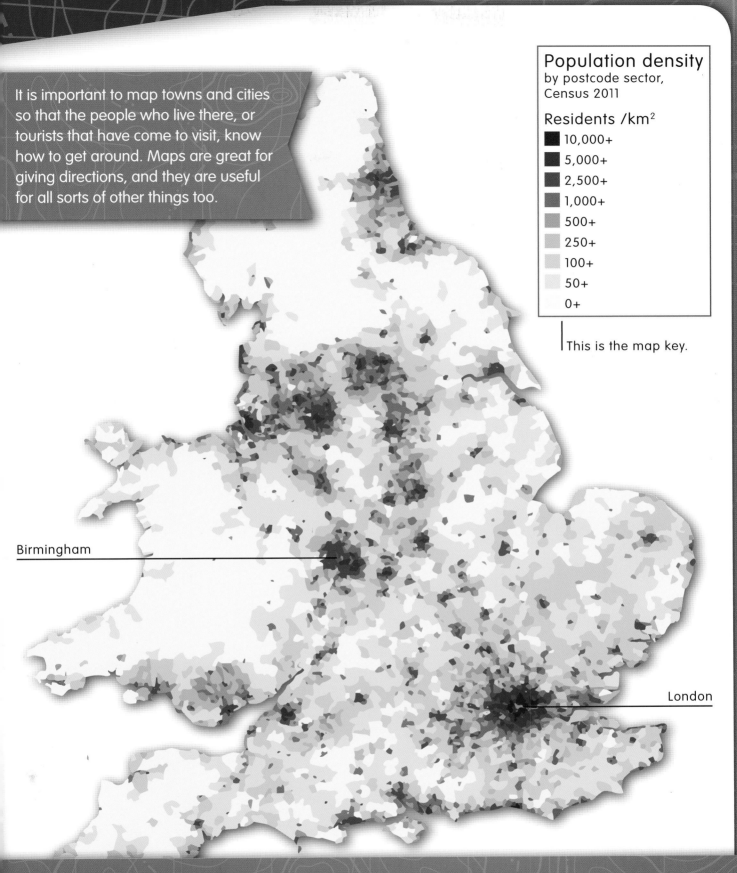

Population density
by postcode sector,
Census 2011

Residents /km^2
- 10,000+
- 5,000+
- 2,500+
- 1,000+
- 500+
- 250+
- 100+
- 50+
- 0+

This is the map key.

Birmingham

London

Maps can be used to show specific pieces of information. For example, this is a population **density** map which shows how many people live in different areas of the UK. The map key tells us that areas in dark red are more densely populated than areas in pink and white. You can see that big cities like London and Birmingham are the most tightly packed with people! Maps are often colour-coded or labelled. Map keys printed alongside the map tell you what these colours and labels mean.

Bird's-Eye-View

Maps are drawn from a bird's-eye-view. This means they are drawn as if looking down at an area from above – like a bird would. Bird's-eye-views of towns and cities help us to see where we are in relation to other places. Many towns will have tourist information maps which have a pin on the street you are on, saying 'you are here'. Knowing your starting point helps you to work out what direction you need to travel to get to where you want to be.

SYMBOLS

A map that showed everything in a particular area would look very cluttered and it would be difficult to pick out the information you need. This is why maps of towns and cities use symbols to show where things are. Depending on the type of map being made, different things will need to be shown. For example, a tourist information map needs to show things such as museums and cafés, while road maps for drivers need to show petrol stations, **toll bridges** and car parks. These symbols often contain numbers, letters or pictures that give extra information.

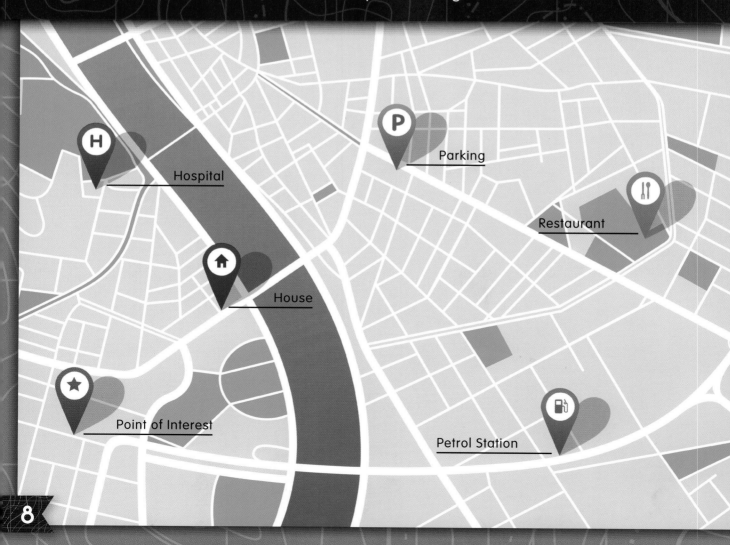

COLOUR CODES

As well as symbols, maps of towns and cities also use colour codes. Colour-coding is especially useful for road maps as they can help drivers tell the difference between different types of road.

This road map of London is colour-coded so drivers can plan their routes in and out of the city. Motorways, like the M1 and the M25, are in green. Motorways are fast, busy roads which usually have three lanes of traffic. Motorways usually run between big cities and allow drivers to travel long distances very fast. On this map, A-roads are in yellow. A-roads are still very fast, but they are smaller than motorways and usually only have two lanes of traffic. They might run between towns rather than cities. The rest of the roads on this map are B-roads. They usually have more twists and turns than motorways and A-roads. These are the kinds of roads you would find in town centres or housing estates. You are likely to live on a B-road.

THE M25 IS A RING-SHAPED MOTORWAY THAT CIRCLES LONDON. IT IS 188 KM LONG!

HOW CITY MAPS ARE MADE

The art of map-making is called cartography. Cartography has a very long history.
Some of the earliest maps were of towns and cities, and were made by climbing to the top of a tall mountain or building and sketching the area. This is called surveying and is a very scientific process. These sketches weren't just pretty drawings; they made use of angles and mathematical calculations to measure the distances between things. We still use these methods today. **Surveyors** make maps of towns and cities using instruments called theodolites, which measure angles and have a telescope so you can measure things far away. Before theodolites, people might have used a graphometer, which is a device for measuring angles and also has a compass.

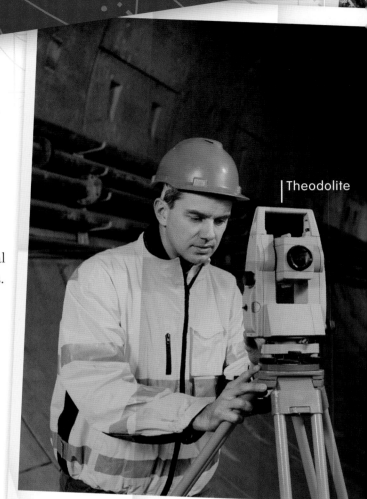
Theodolite

Map of the City of Nippur in Ancient Babylonia

Graphometer

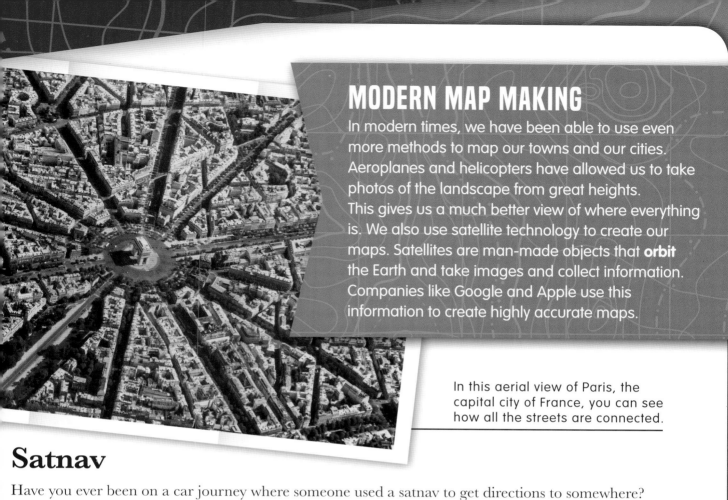

MODERN MAP MAKING

In modern times, we have been able to use even more methods to map our towns and our cities. Aeroplanes and helicopters have allowed us to take photos of the landscape from great heights. This gives us a much better view of where everything is. We also use satellite technology to create our maps. Satellites are man-made objects that **orbit** the Earth and take images and collect information. Companies like Google and Apple use this information to create highly accurate maps.

In this aerial view of Paris, the capital city of France, you can see how all the streets are connected.

Satnav

Have you ever been on a car journey where someone used a satnav to get directions to somewhere? Satnav is short for satellite navigators, and they use something called a global positioning system (GPS). Global positioning systems use signals from satellites to work out the exact location of something on Earth. Satnavs use GPS to show your car moving along the map as you drive.

Satnav

SCALE AND DIRECTION

Scale is the **ratio** between the true size of something and how it is represented on a map. For example, one centimetre (cm) on a map of a town could represent one km in real life. Maps of big places have to be shrunk in order to fit on a fold-out-map or atlas. Having a scale makes sure that – even though it has been shrunk – the reader can still work out the real distance between things.

Map scales are usually printed on a line at the bottom of a map, called a scale bar, and they can be different depending on the size of the area the map is showing. A map of a country might be the same size on paper as a map of a town. This means that one cm on a map of a country would represent a larger distance than it would if it was a map of a town.

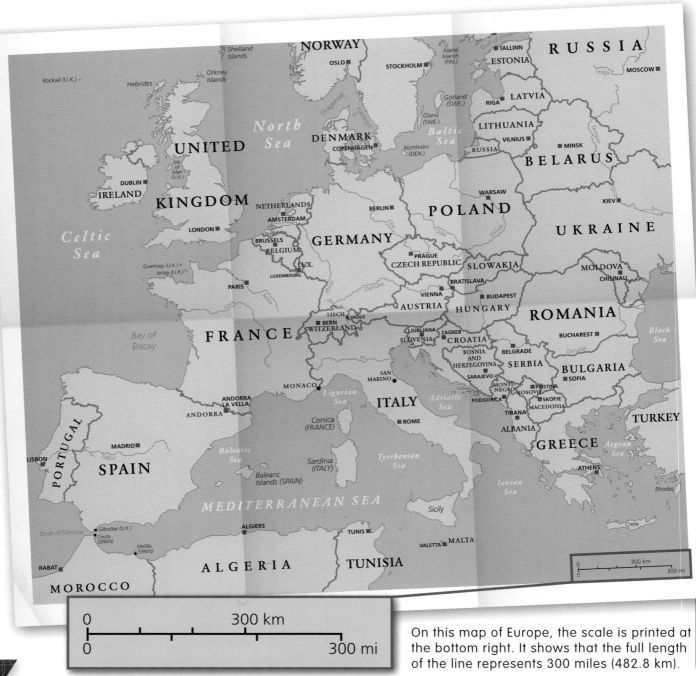

On this map of Europe, the scale is printed at the bottom right. It shows that the full length of the line represents 300 miles (482.8 km).

Map scales are incredibly useful for getting around a city or town because they show you how far things are from each other on a map. If you take a ruler and measure the distance between two places on a map, you can then hold it against the scale bar to find out the distance between them in real life.

Maps also have a drawing of a compass, called a compass rose, printed on them. This tells you which way is north, south, east and west on the map. If you need to travel south but are facing north, it can help to turn your map upside-down so that it matches the direction you are facing.

USING A COMPASS

It can be hard to know which direction you are facing without a real compass. To use a compass you should hold it still and flat in the palm of your hand. Wherever the needle points is north even if it doesn't line up with the 'N' on the compass **dial**. To fix this, you should adjust the dial so that the tip of the needle lines up with the N. Now you can tell which way to turn your map!

BUILDING A CITY

Historical City Maps

Although it may not seem it, the locations of large towns and cities are not a random accident. Usually cities, especially capital cities, are built in certain places for a reason. For example, many capital cities are built around a big river. This is because the first **settlers** who started to build a community there needed a source of water for drinking, cooking and cleaning. Cairo, the capital city of Egypt in Africa, is built around the river Nile. The ancient Egyptians started building their civilisations around the Nile over 4,000 years ago.

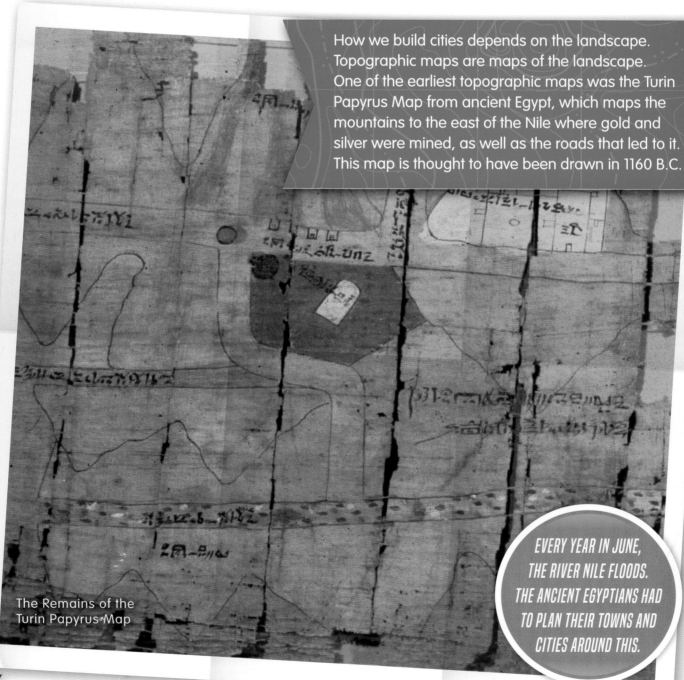

How we build cities depends on the landscape. Topographic maps are maps of the landscape. One of the earliest topographic maps was the Turin Papyrus Map from ancient Egypt, which maps the mountains to the east of the Nile where gold and silver were mined, as well as the roads that led to it. This map is thought to have been drawn in 1160 B.C.

The Remains of the Turin Papyrus Map

EVERY YEAR IN JUNE, THE RIVER NILE FLOODS. THE ANCIENT EGYPTIANS HAD TO PLAN THEIR TOWNS AND CITIES AROUND THIS.

Unplanned Cities

London is a very old city that dates back to when the Romans **occupied** Britain. As London grew larger and larger over hundreds of years, more houses, buildings and streets were added as they were needed and there was no particular plan for their layout.

THE ROMANS CALLED LONDON 'LONDINIUM'.

However, because of the city's long history, there have been many opportunities to change the old, winding roads of London. In 1666, The Great Fire of London started in a small bakery and destroyed over 13,000 houses. The city's narrow streets and tightly-packed wooden houses meant the fire was able to spread very quickly. After the fire, the famous **architect** Christopher Wren wanted to rebuild the streets of London in a grid pattern, and even drew up a map to show his ideas. Unfortunately, the owners of the land wanted to begin rebuilding as soon as possible and didn't have time to consider a new design so, to this day, London remains a tangle of twists and turns.

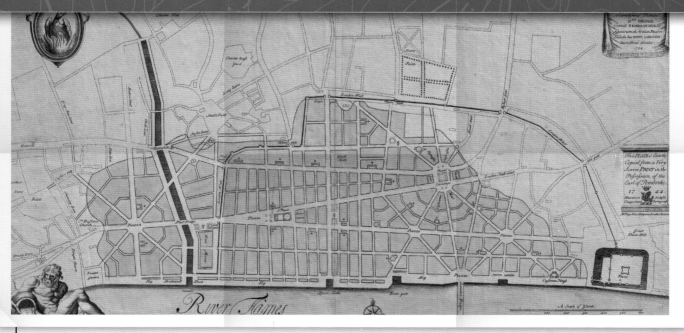

This is what London could have looked like.

Planned Cities

Some cities are planned, and some develop over hundreds of years. New York is a very modern city and much of it was designed on a grid plan. All the roads in Manhattan criss-cross over each other to form a grid. This idea was drawn up on an eight-foot map in 1811 and was called The Commissioner's Plan. Roads that go north to south are called avenues, while roads that go east to west are called streets and are numbered. This makes it easy to give someone directions to a place. For example, The Empire State Building can be found on an avenue between 33rd and 34th street.

THE GRID PLAN IS NOT A MODERN INVENTION. ANCIENT ROMAN CITIES SUCH AS ROME AND POMPEII ALSO USED THE GRID PLAN.

STAY ON THE GRID

As well as using grids to plan the layout of our towns and cities, we also use grids on maps so that we can easily locate things. Maps have vertical (up and down) and horizontal (left to right) lines that cross over to form equally-sized squares in a grid pattern. The vertical lines are called eastings and the horizontal lines are called northings. Each square along the bottom of a map has a letter and each square along the side of the map has a number. You can use these letters and numbers to find a grid reference for anything on the map. For example, the grid reference of the rugby club is [R10]. Why not try it for yourself? Can you find the grid references for the other symbols on this map? What about the hospital?

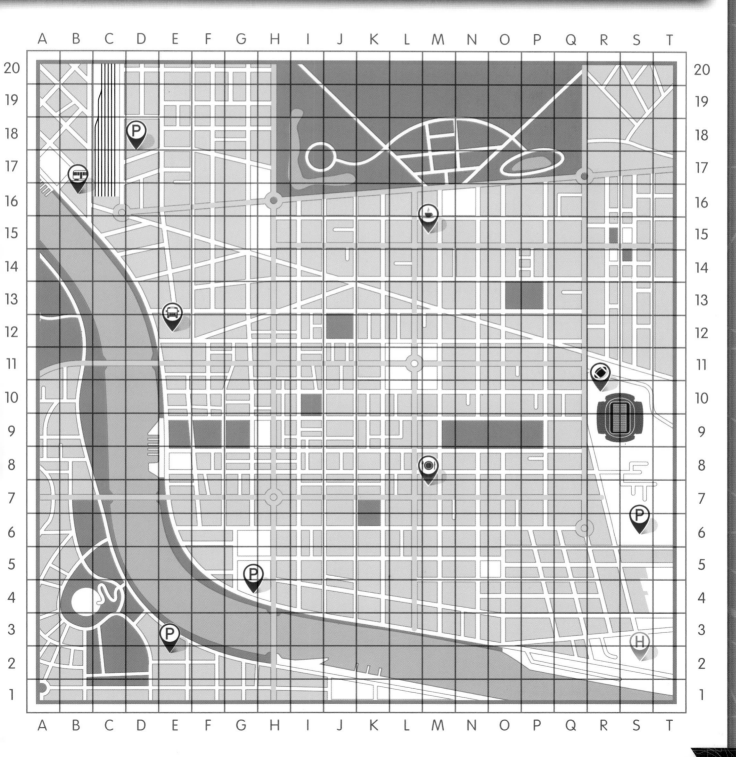

Boats and Bikes

When you think of getting around in a city you might think of underground trains, buses and traffic jams. However, different cities have different ways of getting around. In the city of Amsterdam in the Netherlands, you can travel round the city by boat through a network of man-made waterways called canals. Amsterdam is a very carefully planned city. The area that is now Amsterdam used to be under the sea, but canals were created to drain the land so people could build and farm on it. Making Amsterdam a city where people could live and work took a lot of town planning.

The canals of Amsterdam are organised in **concentric** semi-circles with roads and bridges criss-crossing over them – almost like a spider web!

As well as boats, people in Amsterdam also use bikes to get around. The roads in the city have an extra lane just for bikes, and cyclists can use a map of the city's cycle paths to get around.

AMSTERDAM HAS 160 CANALS!

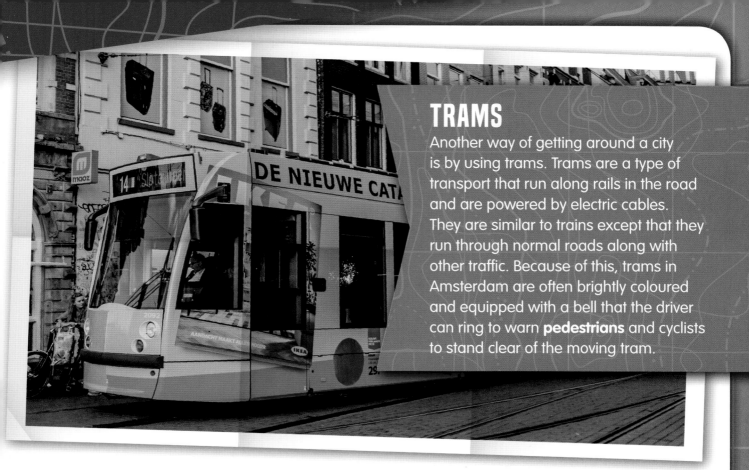

TRAMS

Another way of getting around a city is by using trams. Trams are a type of transport that run along rails in the road and are powered by electric cables. They are similar to trains except that they run through normal roads along with other traffic. Because of this, trams in Amsterdam are often brightly coloured and equipped with a bell that the driver can ring to warn **pedestrians** and cyclists to stand clear of the moving tram.

To help people get around, tram companies design a map which tells you where each of the tram stops are and which route you need to take to get to a particular place. Trams, like buses, are often numbered depending on which route they take. Tram maps also tell you which number tram you need to get.

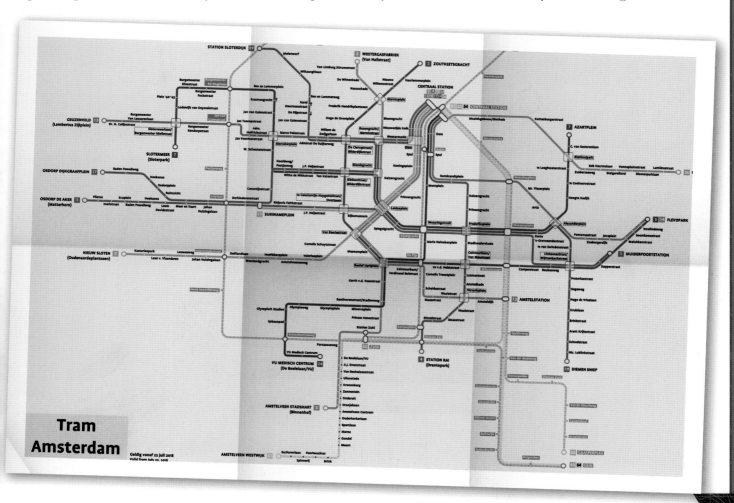

Tram Amsterdam

GOING UNDER

Underground Transport

Cities tend to be very busy, with lots of people living and working in the same area. This often leads to **congested** roads and traffic jams, so it is sometimes quicker to travel underground instead of overground. Many cities such as London, Rome, Moscow and Shanghai have an underground system of trains and stations to help people get around quickly.

MAPPING THE UNDERGROUND

The first stations and tracks for the Underground were built in the 19th century. Although there are now 11 tube lines, back then there were not so many. The stations and lines didn't overlap much, so they could all easily fit onto a map. The Tube map is very important because it shows people which line they need to use and how far away the stations are from each other.

THE LONDON UNDERGROUND IS OFTEN CALLED 'THE TUBE' OR 'THE UNDERGROUND'. THE MAP IS USUALLY CALLED THE TUBE MAP.

London Tube Map, 1908

OLD MAPS, NEW MAPS

The Tube map has changed a lot over the years. In 1931, a man called Harry Beck designed a new map for the Tube that was a lot simpler and easier to read than the older versions. The new map only uses straight lines, and all the stations are drawn as having an equal distance between them. This map was so successful that it is still used today!

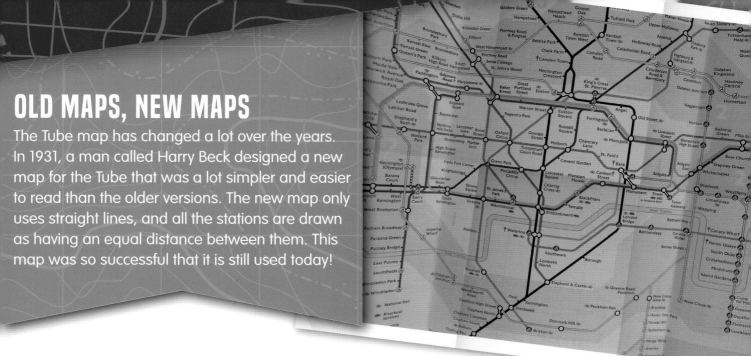

Using Beck's Map

Although it might be easier to plan a journey using the new map, it can be quite confusing if you are trying to learn where places are in London. This is because Beck's design is not geographically accurate – this means that the locations of the Tube stations on the map are only a guide.

Beck also drew many of the stations to be much closer together than they actually are. For example, Marble Arch and Lancaster Gate stations may not look too far apart on the Tube map, but if you look at a map of London, you will see the real distance between them is much farther.

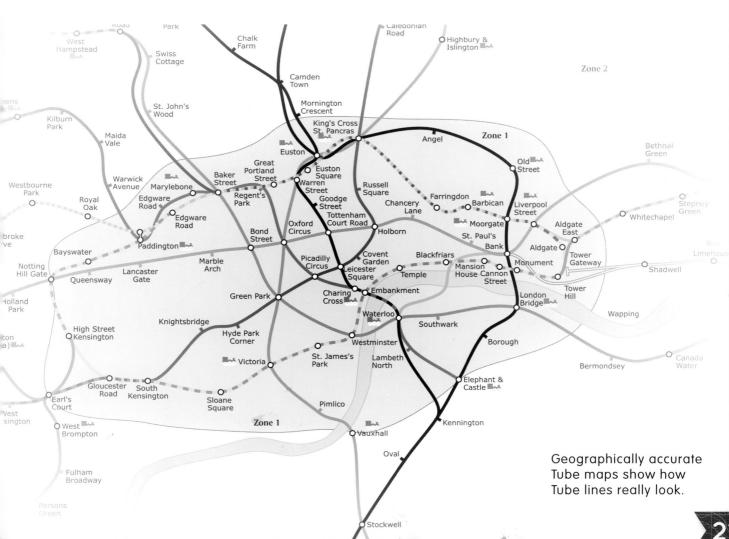

Geographically accurate Tube maps show how Tube lines really look.

TRAFFIC AND
ROAD PLANNING

Lots of people live outside of large towns and cities but work or go to school in the city centre. This means there are large amounts of people travelling in and out of a city at particular times. If your school starts at 8:30 and has 400 pupils, that means there are 400 people and their families travelling to the same place every day. Because of this, roads around your school might get very busy. School bus services are designed to help students get to school on time while reducing the amount of traffic on the roads.

> SOME SCHOOLS THAT ARE BUILT NEAR EACH OTHER START LESSONS AT DIFFERENT TIMES SO THAT PEOPLE AREN'T ALL USING THE SAME ROADS AT ONCE.

Information about the flow of traffic needs to be collected in order to make town planning decisions. For example, if a town needs a new school, it would need to be built somewhere that people were able to get to it. If you were to build a new school directly opposite another school this would affect the flow of traffic and people wouldn't be able to get there in the morning. This is where a type of map called a flow map comes in handy.

As towns and cities grow larger, new roads will need to be built. When town planners want to build a new road through a **residential area,** they have to get something called 'planning permission' from the people who live there. When people buy a house, they own the small piece of land that it is on so they get to decide what happens to it. This means that, if **local authorities** want to build something new there, the residents have to sign an agreement to say it's okay.

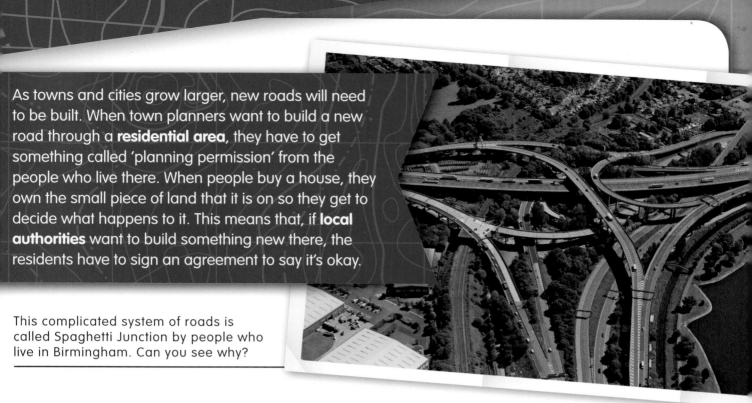

This complicated system of roads is called Spaghetti Junction by people who live in Birmingham. Can you see why?

In China, a dingzihu, or 'nail house', is a house that is still standing because its owner refused to let local authorities or big companies **demolish** it. Nail houses often look very different to their surroundings. They might be towered over by big blocks of flats or they might be found in the middle of a road! House owners are offered a lot of money so they can buy a new house while their old one is being demolished. However, some people still don't want to give up their home.

EDITH MACEFIELD WHO LIVED IN SEATTLE, USA, REFUSED TO ALLOW HER LITTLE FARMHOUSE TO BE DEMOLISHED SO, TO THIS DAY, IT STILL STANDS SQUISHED BETWEEN FIVE-STOREY BUILDINGS.

Guide Books

All maps have different uses and are helpful to different people. If you are on holiday and visiting somewhere for the first time, it might be useful to have a map that shows where landmarks and **points of interest** are. These maps can usually be found in guide books and travel guides. These are books written for tourists and visitors that include information about famous landmarks, popular restaurants, transport routes and places to stay. People often use them to plan their trips and holidays, or to work out how to get from one landmark to the next.

Landmarks in Paris are spread across the city. It is helpful to know what area each one is in so that you can plan your day and decide the best route to each one.

This metro map of Paris shows which station you need to get off at to visit the Louvre museum.

CITYMAPPER

Some tourists and travellers prefer to use smartphone apps instead of traditional guidebooks. One popular app for finding your way around a city is Citymapper. Citymapper does all the hard work for you – it uses GPS technology and information about public transport to 'map' the fastest route to your destination.

Citymapper started in London but can now be used in many cities in the UK and across the world. Once you have entered your destination, you can see whether it is faster to walk, bike, or catch a bus or train. Whichever option you choose – either walking, biking or public transport – your journey will be put onto a map and you will be given instructions and directions to follow.

Citymapper is useful because it is like having lots of guidebooks for different cities all in your pocket – people just need to make sure their smartphone doesn't run out of battery!

CITYMAPPER COVERS CITIES IN NORTH AMERICA, SOUTH AMERICA, EUROPE, ASIA AND AUSTRALIA!

A–Z MAPS

A–Z London

A popular type of map used by both tourists and locals is the A–Z street atlas. A–Z books are popular because they are clear and easy-to-read, and only show important details. The maps are colour-coded and the roads are drawn much wider in comparison to their surroundings than they are in real life. This is because the purpose of a street map is to help people find their way around, so roads and road names are one of the most important features.

All A–Z maps have something called a gazetteer at the back. A gazetteer is a list of things that feature on the map. Depending on the type of map, these things can be geographical features, statistics, and – in the case of A–Z maps – points of interest for tourists and locals. A–Z maps are called this because their gazetteers list points of interest alphabetically, from A–Z.

The first A-Z street atlas was drawn by the cartographer Phyllis Pearsall in the 1930s. The story goes that she had the idea of creating a simple and up-to-date map of London when she got lost on the way to a party after using an old, out-dated map. Her ideas for A-Z maps were very modern. She designed her map to be useful for people in their everyday lives. To this day, hairdressers and shopping centres are more likely to be featured on the map than statues and tourist landmarks.

Activity

1. If you were making a map of your local area, what points of interest would you want to include? Can you list them alphabetically?

2. Why not have a go at designing a map of the town, village or city you live in? Do you remember all the street names and how they connect to each other?

EARLY A–Z MAPS WERE BLACK AND WHITE, BUT NOWADAYS A-ROADS ARE ORANGE AND B-ROADS ARE YELLOW. THIS HAS LED TO TAXI DRIVERS REFERRING TO THEM AS 'ORANGES AND LEMONS'.

MAP GAMES

Monopoly

Monopoly is a game based on a map of a town or city. The squares around the edge of the board all represent a different street in the city. Players roll a dice and move around the board, each time landing on a different street. You can buy property and hotels on your streets which means a person has to pay you money each time they land on your street. If you land on their street you have to pay money to them. This money is called rent.

SIM CITY

Sim City is a videogame where you can plan and build your own city. The aim of the game is to build a city with residential zones, industrial zones and commercial zones for the city's citizens – called Sims – to live, work and shop in. The player is given a small **budget** to start with and a blank map to start building on. Your city can be viewed on a map in bird's-eye-view but you can also view your city from the ground.

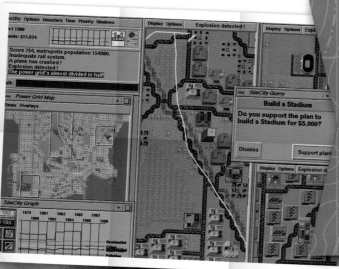

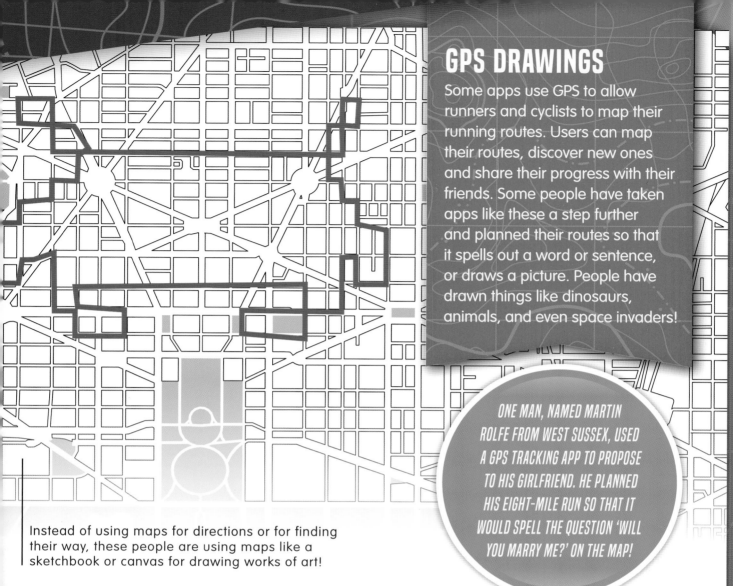

Some apps use GPS to allow runners and cyclists to map their running routes. Users can map their routes, discover new ones and share their progress with their friends. Some people have taken apps like these a step further and planned their routes so that it spells out a word or sentence, or draws a picture. People have drawn things like dinosaurs, animals, and even space invaders!

ONE MAN, NAMED MARTIN ROLFE FROM WEST SUSSEX, USED A GPS TRACKING APP TO PROPOSE TO HIS GIRLFRIEND. HE PLANNED HIS EIGHT-MILE RUN SO THAT IT WOULD SPELL THE QUESTION 'WILL YOU MARRY ME?' ON THE MAP!

Instead of using maps for directions or for finding their way, these people are using maps like a sketchbook or canvas for drawing works of art!

Top Secret?

In 2018, a fitness app called Strava, which people can use to map their running or cycling routes, launched a new feature. Heatmaps showed all the exercise data shared by its members all over the world. Popular areas or routes glow brightly on the map. However, it also accidentally showed where many secret US military bases were too.

Lots of soldiers were using the app to track their fitness while away, and the maps were so detailed that they even showed the internal paths and roads in the military bases, causing security problems. Soldiers are now trained to switch off this setting and be more careful what they share!

ACTIVITY

QUICK QUIZ

1. What is the name for a person whose job it is to create maps?

2. What does a 'bird's-eye-view' mean?

3. What instrument do surveyors use to measure angles?

4. What does GPS stand for?

5. What was the name of the architect who wanted to rebuild London's streets in a grid pattern after the Great Fire of London?

6. Can you name three methods of transport that people use to get around in Amsterdam?

7. When was the map of the London Underground designed?

8. What tool can you use to find out which direction you are facing?

9. Which map app can tell you the fastest route to your destination using GPS?

10. What colour are A-roads on an A–Z map?

GLOSSARY

architect	someone who designs buildings
budget	a set amount of money allocated to a project
concentric	circles or spheres which have the same centre but are differently sized
congested	blocked or filled, especially roads
demolish	tear down or destroy
density	how tightly-packed something is
diagrams	drawings that are used for technical purposes
dial	a disc with numbers and a pointer to show a measurement
features	a part or quality of something, especially to identify it
landmarks	identifying features of a place, usually permanent
local authorities	local governments of a particular place
occupied	taken over by another ruler or government
orbit	the path that an object makes around a larger object in space
pedestrians	people travelling on foot and not in a vehicle
points of interest	places of particular note
precincts	areas of a city looked after by one police unit
ratio	relation or comparison between two numbers
residential area	place in which people live
settlers	people who start to live in a new area of land
squared	the result of a number multiplied by itself
surveyors	people who study land to be built on
toll bridges	bridges where a fee is collected if you want to cross

INDEX

Aberdeenshire  COUNCIL

Aberdeenshire Libraries
www.aberdeenshire.gov.uk/libraries

2 1 JUL 2022

- 6 APR 2023

3 0 SEP 2023

2 5 NOV 2023

Aberdeenshire

3229765